First World War
and Army of Occupation
War Diary
France, Belgium and Germany

34 DIVISION
102 Infantry Brigade
Herefordshire Regiment
1/1st Battalion
1 June 1918 - 30 April 1919

WO95/2462/3

The Naval & Military Press Ltd
www.nmarchive.com
Published in association with The National Archives

Published by

The Naval & Military Press Ltd

Unit 10 Ridgewood Industrial Park,

Uckfield, East Sussex,

TN22 5QE England

Tel: +44 (0) 1825 749494

www.naval-military-press.com

www.nmarchive.com

This diary has been reprinted in facsimile from the original. Any imperfections are inevitably reproduced and the quality may fall short of modern type and cartographic standards.

© **Crown Copyright**
Images reproduced by permission of The National Archives, London, England, 2015.

Contents

Document type	Place/Title	Date From	Date To
Heading	34th Division 102nd Infy Bde 1-1st Bn Hereford Regt 1918 Jan-1919 Apl From E.G.Y.P.T. 53 Div 158 Bde		
War Diary	N,14.C.	01/06/1918	01/06/1918
War Diary	Hawk Hill Ramallah	02/06/1918	02/06/1918
War Diary	Enab	03/06/1918	03/06/1918
War Diary	Latron	04/06/1918	04/06/1918
War Diary	Surafend	05/06/1918	06/06/1918
War Diary	Kantara Kilo 5.	07/06/1918	15/06/1918
War Diary	Kantara	16/06/1918	17/06/1918
War Diary	On Board HMT. Kaiser.I.Hind.	18/06/1918	22/06/1918
War Diary	Toronto On Train	23/06/1918	30/06/1918
Miscellaneous	1/1st. Herefordshire Regt. Appendices To The War Diary for the month of June 1917		
War Diary	Oost. Cappel (Les Cinq Chemins) France.	01/07/1918	07/07/1918
War Diary	Schools Camp St. Janter Biezen. Flanders.	08/07/1918	10/07/1918
War Diary	Schools Camp St Janter Biezen.	11/07/1918	13/07/1918
War Diary	Cormette Camp	14/07/1918	15/07/1918
War Diary	Rowsbrugge	16/07/1918	17/07/1918
War Diary	Borest.	18/07/1918	20/07/1918
War Diary	Poiseux.	21/07/1918	23/07/1918
War Diary	Field.	23/07/1918	31/07/1918
Miscellaneous	1st Herefordshire Regt.		
War Diary	Field.	01/08/1918	04/08/1918
War Diary	Sill-Le-Long	05/08/1918	06/08/1918
War Diary	In Train	07/08/1918	07/08/1918
War Diary	Zeggers Capel	08/08/1918	13/08/1918
War Diary	Hezeel	14/08/1918	19/08/1918
War Diary	Proven	20/08/1918	21/08/1918
War Diary	Siege Camp Div Resv	22/08/1918	27/08/1918
War Diary	Road Camp	28/08/1918	28/08/1918
War Diary	Cormette	29/08/1918	31/08/1918
Miscellaneous	1/1st Herefordshire Rgt Appendix to the War Diary for Month of August 1918		
War Diary	St. Omer	01/09/1918	01/09/1918
War Diary	M12 C 82 Div Res	02/09/1918	02/09/1918
War Diary	Front Line	03/09/1918	07/09/1918
War Diary	Rest N 15	08/09/1918	13/09/1918
War Diary	M 16 B 10.7	14/09/1918	14/09/1918
War Diary	Mb. 10.7. Div Res.	15/09/1918	15/09/1918
War Diary	Front Line	16/09/1918	20/09/1918
War Diary	Support Line	21/09/1918	22/09/1918
War Diary	Div. Res	23/09/1918	28/09/1918
War Diary	Bde Res	29/09/1918	30/09/1918
Miscellaneous	War Diary Appendix September 1918		
War Diary	Wytchaete	01/10/1918	01/10/1918
War Diary	Nr Houtem	02/10/1918	02/10/1918
War Diary	Support Line	03/10/1918	07/10/1918
War Diary	Div Resv P. 3.a. 5.9.	08/10/1918	12/10/1918
War Diary	Support Line	13/10/1918	15/10/1918
War Diary	Line.	15/10/1918	16/10/1918

War Diary	Menin Front Line.	16/10/1918	16/10/1918
War Diary	Bde. Resv.	17/10/1918	19/10/1918
War Diary	On Move	19/10/1918	19/10/1918
War Diary	St Anne	20/10/1918	22/10/1918
War Diary	On. Move	23/10/1918	23/10/1918
War Diary	Front Line	24/10/1918	25/10/1918
War Diary	Field	25/10/1918	26/10/1918
War Diary	Move	27/10/1918	29/10/1918
War Diary	Harlebeke	30/10/1918	31/10/1918
Miscellaneous	War Diary Appendix October 1918		
War Diary	Harlebeke	01/11/1918	01/11/1918
War Diary	Div Resv.	02/11/1918	03/11/1918
War Diary	Moorseele Corps Resv	04/11/1918	13/11/1918
War Diary	On Move	14/11/1918	16/11/1918
War Diary	On Move	16/11/1918	16/11/1918
War Diary	Renaix	17/11/1918	17/11/1918
War Diary	On Move	18/11/1918	18/11/1918
War Diary	Floebecq	19/11/1918	30/11/1918
Miscellaneous	1st. Bn. The Herefordshire Regiment. Appendices To The War Diary For The Month Of November, 1918		
War Diary	Flobecq	01/12/1918	11/12/1918
War Diary	On Move	12/12/1918	12/12/1918
War Diary	Silly	13/12/1918	13/12/1918
War Diary	On Move	14/12/1918	14/12/1918
War Diary	Silly	13/12/1918	13/12/1918
War Diary	On Move	14/12/1918	14/12/1918
War Diary	Soignes	15/12/1918	15/12/1918
War Diary	On Move	16/12/1918	19/12/1918
War Diary	Fosse	20/12/1918	31/12/1918
Miscellaneous	1st. Bn. The Herefordshire Regiment. Appendices To The War Diary for Month of Decr. 1918		
War Diary	Fosse Belgium.	01/01/1919	23/01/1919
War Diary	Beuel. Germany	24/01/1919	29/01/1919
War Diary	Beuel	30/01/1919	30/01/1919
War Diary	Siegburg	31/01/1919	31/01/1919
War Diary	Seelscheid		
Miscellaneous	Appendices App I Casualties		
Heading	34 Division 102 Infantry Brigade 1 Battalion Herefordshire Reg Feb 1919 Missing.		
War Diary	Siegburg	01/03/1919	22/03/1919
War Diary	Germany	23/03/1919	30/03/1919
War Diary	Ath. Belgium	31/03/1919	30/04/1919

34TH DIVISION
102ND INFY BDE

1-1ST BN HEREFORD REGT
~~JUN - DEC 1918~~

1918 JUN — 1919 APL

FROM EGYPT
53 DIV 158 BDE

SECRET

WAR DIARY or **INTELLIGENCE SUMMARY**

Army Form C. 2118.

1/1 HEREFORDSHIRE

JUNE 1918

Place	Date	Hour	Summary of Events and Information	Remarks and references to Appendices
N.H.C.	JUNE 1	0800	Bn moved off. Joined with by Div Band and marched to HAWK HILL V16, and Went into bivouac for the night. Coy's carried out their Bn Ou Rounds.	TELFIT /
HAWK HILL RAMALLAH	2	0445	Bn moved off. Halted at BETUNIA for breakfast, and proceeded to ENAB, and bivouaced for the night.	40.000. PALESTINE Sheet 3
ENAB	3	0500	Bn moved to LATRON, and went into bivouac to #/11 GURKHS Brigade.	IV VI VII
LATRON	4		Bn marched to SURAFEND.	/
SURAFEND	5		Bn rested and loaded on Swifts stores ammun[iti]ons vehicles	63360.
"	6		Bn marched to LYDD and entrained at 1945 and 2145. Appx	
KANTARA	7		arriving at KANTARA at 0900 and 1100 and proceeded to camp at KILO 5.	I li IV
KILO 5.	8		Refitting, washing clothes, training	
"	9		As " 8th	
"	10		As " 9th. Draft arrived to complete to Establishment.	
"	11		As " 10th Bn passed through a Gas Chamber	
"	12		As " 11th	
"	13		Refitting, washing, and bathing	
"	14		As " 13th	
"	15		" " 14th.	

SECRET.

WAR DIARY 1/1 HEREFORDSHIRE Rgt. Army Form C. 2118.
or
INTELLIGENCE SUMMARY.

(Erase heading not required.)

JUNE 1918

Instructions regarding War Diaries and Intelligence Summaries are contained in F. S. Regs., Part II. and the Staff Manual respectively. Title pages will be prepared in manuscript.

Place	Date	Hour	Summary of Events and Information	Remarks and references to Appendices
KANTARA	JUNE 16	1930	Bn moved out of camp and proceeded to KANTARA WEST station entraining at 2200.	
	17	0730	Arrived at N°20 Quay ALEXANDRIA, and embarked on H.M.T. KAISER-I-HIND.	
on board H.M.T. KAISER-I-HIND	18	0730	Troopship went into outer harbour.	
		1300	Ship sailed as part of a convoy, escorted by JAPANESE destroyers.	
"	19		At Sea	
"	20		At Sea	
"	21		At Sea. 1130 Stood to, torpedo fired enemy submarine passed astern. 1300 entered TARANTO outer harbour. 1700 entered inner harbour, unloaded baggage all night.	
"	22		Bn disembarked into lighters, and landed at Pier, — went into hutments near.	
TORANTO	23	2230	Bn entrained. 2 Pass coaches, 29 goods trucks, 1ration, 1baggage, 1M.O.	
On TRAIN	24		On Train	
"	25		. . . .	
"	26			
"	27			
"	28			
"	29			
"	30		arrived at PROVEN, detrained and marched to OOST CAPPEL, LES CINQ CHEMINS Coys to Thillels, barns and huinents.	

1/1st. Herefordshire Regt.

APPENDICES TO THE WAR DIARY for the month of JUNE 1917

APPENDIX 1 - CASUALTIES :

	Officers	Other Ranks
Killed	-	-
Wounded	-	4
Missing	-	-
Sick Admitted	3	85
	3	89

APPENDIX 2 - REINFORCEMENTS :

	Officers	Other Ranks
From England	-	-
From Hospital (sick)	-	93
From Hospital (wounded)	1	37
Various	2	52
	3	182

APPENDIX 3 - HEALTH OF TROOPS :

Daily percentage of sick :-

'A' Coy. - 1.8   Battalion   'B' Coy. - 2.1
                    Average
'B' Coy. - 1.8   2.0   'D' Coy. - 2.3

APPENDIX 4 - OFFICER CASUALTIES :

2/Lieut.P.T.Raymond   -   To Hospital 11/6/18
Lieut.W.F.Bushell   -   To Hospital 28/6/18
2/Lieut.A.P.D.Michael -   To Hospital 28/6/18
2/Lieut.H.Peake   -   From Hospital 13/6/16
2/Lieut. H.Waters   -   From Base   4/6/18
2/Lieut.A.P.D.Michael -   From Base   8/6/18

-:-

SECRET July 1918

WAR DIARY
or
INTELLIGENCE SUMMARY.

Army Form C. 2118.
1/1st HEREFORDSHIRE REGT
B E F

Place	Date	Hour	Summary of Events and Information	Remarks and references to Appendices
OOST CAPPEL (LES CINQ CHEMINS) FRANCE	1st		Equipment drawn and issued. Store tent erected. 20 additional Lewis Guns drawn.	
do.	2nd		Re. organization of Bn. to conform with lower establishment	
do	3rd		" " " "	
do.	4th		Inspection by G.O.C. 34th Division.	
do	5th		Company and specialist training	
do	6th		" " "	
	7th	0730	Bn. moved by march route to Schools Camp, ST. JAN TER BIEZEN, arriving 1130.	
Schools Camp. ST. JAN TER BIEZEN. FLANDERS.	8th		Company training and administration.	
	9th	10.30. 22.00.	Bn. on rest of Bde. was inspected by Lincd. Eleven and Corps Comdr. "Br." proceeded to take up its position as BDE. Reserve at about M.W.d. Withdrew at 0200 - 1017.	
do	10th		Coy. Administration. 3 Bombards caused through Gas hut.	

WAR DIARY or INTELLIGENCE SUMMARY

Army Form C. 2118.

Unit: 1st West Yorkshire Regt.

Place	Date	Hour	Summary of Events and Information	Remarks and references to Appendices
Schools Camp, St Martin's Camp, Boulogne	Feb 11th 1918		Company & Specialist training.	
do	12th		Training modified owing to inclement weather.	
do	13th	0400	No Company enclave broken. Entrained at MENDINGHAM for ST. OMER 14.45. Remaining 2 Coys & Bn. H.Q. entrained at 14.45, arriving ST. OMER 16.30. Proceeded to Camp by march route. Transport and baggage by road.	
CORMETTE CAMP	14th	1000	Commenced Musketry course.	
do	15th		Musketry continued until 10.00, when move orders were received. First seven and billeting party proceeded in advance to ROUSBRUGGE. Bn. entrained at ST. OMER at 16.00, arriving ROUSBRUGGE 20.30. Bn. quartered in huts near Rousbrugge Station.	
ROUSBRUGGE	16th		Move orders received 04.30. Bn. entrained in two parties at ROUSBRUGGE at 21.00 and 02.00-18th respectively. H.Q. on first train.	
	17th		On train. Arrived PAR VINCKEM 23.25 and detrained. Marched away at 23.50.	
BOREST	18th	0600	Arrived BOREST, covering distance of 14 or 15 miles. Men entrained well, only 4 falling out. These rejoined the Bn. an hour after its arrival. A, C, D. Coys billeted at 0700. A party was left at station to detrain transport. This arrived BOREST 07.30. B. Coy, who came on later train, arrived BOREST 10.50.	

Secret. Y.S. Leinster Regt. Army Form C. 2118.

WAR DIARY
or
INTELLIGENCE SUMMARY.
(Erase heading not required.)

Instructions regarding War Diaries and Intelligence Summaries are contained in F.S. Regs., Part II. and the Staff Manual respectively. Title pages will be prepared in manuscript.

Place	Date 1918	Hour	Summary of Events and Information	Remarks and references to Appendices
BORGST	18th		Medical Inspection and Bathing during afternoon.	
do	19th	00.30	Received orders to Entrain to Engine at daylight. Later, received orders to entrain at 06.00. Transport to travel Brigaded to new area.	
		10.00	Arrived VERMOISE. C.O. went forward to find Billets. Everyone settled in by 12.00.	
do	20th	16.30	Mop. indication in fighting order. Noon orders received. Bn. pioneers at 19.30 and marched to Engine rendezvous - VEZ. arriving 21.00. Bn. moved to Brigade. Bn. awaiting orders. During halt a violent thunderstorm burst, lasting nearly half an hour.	
		11.40	Left VEZ., march route, 10th Major guiding Column. Various halts necessitated by cross traffic.	
POISEUX	21st	07.00	Arrived POISEUX. Billets rutted down by 08.00. March occupied 12 hours. No other Lanks full out. 2/Lieut Michael as I.O. and 2/Lieut Ward, T.O. proceeded at 15.30 to reconnoitre route to LONGPORT.	
do	22nd	07.30	Bn. aroused to a night rendezvous, a distance of 14 kilo from starting point, arriving at 14.45. All movement was camouflaged by walking through the woods. Night march commenced 21.00. Passing point line 23.00. Relief of 58th French Bon. completed by 23.50.	
	23rd	04.45	Preliminary attack orders received. Attack commenced 07.40 in following order :- B&C, firing line, D in support to an left flank, A in	

D. D. & L., London, E.C. (A804) Wt. W1771/M231 750,000 5/17 Sch. 32 Forms/C2118/14

WAR DIARY or INTELLIGENCE SUMMARY

Army Form C. 2118.

Scott

Turkoplanies Regt.

Place	Date	Hour	Summary of Events and Information	Remarks and references to Appendices
FIELD.	Feb 6.1916 / 23rd	0900	Very heavy shell fire experienced immediately more commenced. High standing corn found difficult to move through, and wire being control almost impossible. Casualties from enemy M.G. occurred before attack had engaged enemy yard. Attack held up at 1300, from point of deployment. Owing mainly to units on either flank failing to advance at all. We maintained ground gained until after night fall, when they were relieved by 4 Cheshire Regt. and 17th Cheshire Regt on left. Casualties heavy, approx 8 officers, 230 O.R. Continuous shelling of whole line during night, making search for and evacuation of wounded difficult. Gas shells experienced by Bn. for first time during this attack.	
do.	24th	DAWN	Cheshires consequently took over whole line, Bn withdrawing to reserve area to reorganise into two companies under Capt. Carlson and Lieut Grover. 6th Cheshires came to Bn HQ., experienced gratification at the part played by the Battalion in the operations, explaining that 103 O.R. were the only unit to reach any ground in the corps area. During evening, reserve area constantly shelled heavily during day. Casualties, 2 O.R. killed, 4 wounded. Enemy airplane fired on our lines.	
do.	25th			

WAR DIARY or INTELLIGENCE SUMMARY

Army Form C. 2118.

1/1st Nottinghamshire Regt.

Place	Date	Hour	Summary of Events and Information	Remarks and references to Appendices
FIELD	July 1915 26th		Enemy shelling most of the day. M.O. first came to dressing dugout & was totally slightly by the war. On arrival it was found to be part of a shell and uninhabitable. He returned to its original dugout.	
do.	27th		Situation unchanged. Estimated casualties to date 10 Officer casualties, 98 O.R. Killed, 206 Wounded, 9 missing. Received orders from B.G. that we were to be relieved by French Battalion DE TARBES. They replied did not turn up in evening.	
	28th		DETAILS to O.C.'s above, and we were relieved by French Colonel Bn. Relf Complete Bn. & O.R. marched to new Bivouac area arriving about 0500. Handed to W.K. informed and B. now were detailed and ordered to remain behind when the Bn. moved.	
	29th	21.00 00.30	Received order to send at 23.05. On getting on the line of march, myself out 8 men to Quite back, and consequently we were half up for half an hour being shelled the road, but luckily none had effect. Met O/C French Bn who was to take us to new division. Out (The battalion, with most that we had to look out for older for Quicker & luckily kit the unit our many heavy shells were dropped	
		10.30	In our area during night time, but no material damage done. First order from Bde to enemy the Cam trench system, to be closer to our firing line. On arrival we found the firing only just in front, then the whole Bn. set to work to consolidate the system.	
	30th		Enemy entered a pair movement of Sa Valley westerners and Normandy, causing two casualties San Louis. Air line was prolonged to a distance of 500, owing most out a work. Of drop cord activities. Patrols during day, & R. 14 Toda.	
	31st		Noted to act to out that them whatever Enemy shelled line very vigorously from 23.00 to 23.00	

H.M. Laurence
Lieut. Col. Comdg. 1/1 Nottinghamshire Regt.

1st Herefordshire Regt.

Appendices to the War Diary for Month of July, 1918

Appendix I - Casualties

	Officers	Other Ranks
Killed	1	35
Wounded	10	246
Missing	-	18
Sick Admitted	1	63
	12	362

Appendix II - Reinforcements

	Officers	Other Ranks
From England	5	-
From Hospital	1	56
Various	-	-
	6	56

Appendix III - Health of Troops

Daily %age of Sick.

A - 1.8   Bn %age   C - 2.4
B - 2.0   2.1.   D - 2.2

Admissions:-

A - 18   Total - 63   C - 18
B - 12   D - 15

Officer Casualties:-

Increase
- 2/Lieut A.P.D. Michael from Hosp.
- " P.L. Richards " Eng'd
- " L.G. Jones " "
- " W.H. Hughes " "
- " H.J. Baynes " "
- " J.C. Murphy " "

Decrease
- Capt F.A. Trumper - wounded
- Lieut J.P. Rogers "
- 2/L. H.H. Palmer "
- " L.G. Jones "
- " H.J. Baynes "
- " W.H. Hughes "
- " H.W. Hunt "
- " A.P.D. Michael "
- Lieut J.P. Sworder D.o.W.
- Lieut H. Waters to UK for M.G. Training

Secret.

Army Form C. 2118.

WAR DIARY 1st HEREFORDSHIRE REG.T
or
INTELLIGENCE SUMMARY. 102 Bde.
34 DIV

Aug 1918.

Instructions regarding War Diaries and Intelligence Summaries are contained in F.S. Regs., Part II. and the Staff Manual respectively. Title pages will be prepared in manuscript.
(Erase heading not required.)

Place	Date	Hour	Summary of Events and Information	Remarks and references to Appendices
FIELD.	Aug.1	a.m.	Intense French artillery fire during night, enemy replied.	REF: MAPS. OULCHY-LE-CHATEAU. HARTENNES OULCHY.
		4:45 a.m.	Our barrage began on enemies position.	
		5-15	Bn advanced in rear of 103 Bde. Objective being BUCY-LE-BRAS. During this advance Major A.G.R. Whitehouse, M.C. was killed by a small party of enemy, who suddenly appeared at short range (120x) right of fins front Bn. Bn H.Q. party & this was a complete surprise as 1/2 Bde. had only just passed over the area.	APPDX I to III
		11/35	Bn reached point 189 1260x North of BEUGNEUX, and dug in. Further advance being held up by heavy M.G. fire from woods 600x South West of BUCY-LE-BRAS.	
			Bn relieved by 103 Bde, & concentrated as support of Pt-189.	
		8-10	Enemy counter attack signalled by Verilites, Bn more upper, support trenches at Pt 189 under heavy enemy shelling.	
		11-0	Bn relieved by 1/7 Cheshire R.; and retired to PARIS French System.	
	2		Bn remained as Bde Res.r Salvage & burial parties sent out.	
	3		As for 2nd inst.	
	4	a.m. 9-0	Bn moved to CHATEAU-THIERY road and entrained, proceeding to NANTIEUL arriving 6pm, marched to billets in SILLY-LE-LONG 1st Hereford Reformed	

SECRET.

Army Form C. 2118.

WAR DIARY
or
INTELLIGENCE SUMMARY.

AUG 1918.

1st HEREFORDSHIRE REGT
102 Bde
34 DIV

(Erase heading not required.)

Instructions regarding War Diaries and Intelligence Summaries are contained in F.S. Regs., Part II. and the Staff Manual respectively. Title pages will be prepared in manuscript.

Place	Date	Hour	Summary of Events and Information	Remarks and references to Appendices
SILLE-LE-LONG	AUG 5		Bn cleaning up, resting & Admin work.	
"	6	3-0 pm	Bn marched to PLESSIS (BELLEVILLE) and entrained 4pm. Train left 6pm, stopped at U.S. for tea, at 10pm.	
En Train	7		Train stopped NOYELLE for breakfast 9am, arrived BERGUES at 5pm. Bn marched to Ridells about 1 mile South of ZEGGERS CAPEL.	
ZEGGERS CAPEL	8		Bn reorganizing and Admin work.	
"	9		As in 8th. CO proceeded on leave to UK	
"	10		Coy training, inter Pl. talks.	
"	11		Sunday Divine Service, H.C. 3 Offrs 15 ORs draft arrived.	
"	12		Bn inf Min (30x) range. Draft 2 1 H.O. OR arrived Coys Commdrs inspected drafts who had lately joined. (Draft of 50 OR arrived (very young, many under 19yrs)	
"	13	7.30	Bn marched Brigaded to HEZEEL, B.O.C. 34 Div acralched Bdg march. feast.	
HEZEEL	14		Bn admin & Coy training	
"	15		Bde classes furnied 9 off 90 NCO's & men attended. Bn continued Coy training 2 Coys fired Min (30x) range	
"	16		As in 15th.	
"	17		As in 16. Bde sports: Bn I.O.H: won cup presented by B.G.C. 102 Bde	

SECRET

WAR DIARY or INTELLIGENCE SUMMARY.

(Erase heading not required.)

1st HEREFORDSHIRE Army Form C. 2118.
102 Bde
34 DIV.
Aug 1918

Place	Date	Hour	Summary of Events and Information	Remarks and references to Appendices
HEZEELE	Aug 18		Sunday, Bgde Church Parade. Shorts etc Tug-o-War won by Bn.	MAP Ref. BELGIUM FRANCE
	19	8.0 am	Bn marched Brigades to PROVEN. (Pigeon Camp).	
PROVEN	20		Bn training.	SHEET 27 1/40,000
	21	9.30	Bn moved off and marched to SIEGE CAMP B.27.a+6. (Sheet 28) and relieved 1/4 KOYLI. Bn formed pal. D Bde in Div Res. Officers reconnoitred "ROME FARM" Switch line."	SHEET 28 1/20,000
SIEGE CAMP Div Res	22		All Officers & NCO's reconnoitred GREEN LINE, enemy shelled area (slightly) during night.	
"	23		Bn trained, Reconnaissance of FRONTLINE made by Officers & NCO's	
"	24		As in 23rd. KAAIE and DICKEBUSH positions reconnoitred.	
"	25		Sunday. Rly DS. further reconnaissance carried out.	
"	26		Bn working in trenches under RE. CO returned from leave.	
"	27		Bn relieved by 1/4 Yrk Rgt. Bn entrained on light Rly. in two trains at 16.30, arrived LANCASTER, siding and marched to ROAD CAMP. St JAN-TER-BIEZEN.	
ROAD CAMP	28	6.15	Bn marched to PROVEN station, and entrained arriving St OMER 1-4-5 marched to CORMETTE CAMP. 3½ moved by road in two days to reconnoitre KEMMEL area a 24 hours reconnaissance was carried out from SCHERPENBERG Gemete.	

SECRET

1st HEREFORDSHIRE Regt
Aug 1918
102 Bde
34 DIV

WAR DIARY
or
INTELLIGENCE SUMMARY
Army Form C. 2118.

(Erase heading not required.)

Instructions regarding War Diaries and Intelligence Summaries are contained in F. S. Regs., Part II. and the Staff Manual respectively. Title pages will be prepared in manuscript.

Place	Date	Hour	Summary of Events and Information	Remarks and references to Appendices
CORMETTE	Aug/18			Ref. MAPS FRANCE 27 A SE 1/20000
"	30		Bn Admnst work. Trenches dug around tents. Coy training. CO Coy Comdrs rejoined Bn. Musketry on range near Coys carried out. Appl: & Rapid at-200x & Appl: at 300x.	
"	31		Bn under orders to move at short notice.	

H Lawrence Lieut Col
Comdg
1st Herefords Regt

1. Herefordshire Regt.

Appendices to the War Diary for Month of AUGUST 1918

Appendix I Casualties.

	Officers	Other Ranks
Killed	2	7
Wounded	1	29
Missing		-
Sick Admitted		55
	3	91

Appendix II Reinforcements.

	Officers	Other Ranks
From England & Base	18	406
Hospital		33
Various		-
	18	439

Appendix III – Health of Troops.

Daily % of Sick

A 1.7 Bn Average 1.9 C 2.0
B 2.1   D 1.8

Admissions:—

A 12   C 15
B 17 Total 55 D 11

Officer Casualties.

Increase
2 Lieut T. Frazermith
" E.J. Payne
" J. Mitchell
" M.G.C. Blackmore
" N.E. Edwards
" R. Bonnett
" R. Moses
" E. Sully
" G.A.H. Stimming
" E.C. Gates
" W.P. Price
" J.E. Middleton
" G.J.L. Pelham
" H. Berkmere
" A.J. Edwards

Decrease
Maj. A.G.R. Whitehouse MC (K)
2/Maj. H.R.D. Fraser (K)
2 Lieut B.L. Richards (W)

2 Lt M.J. Clarke
     D.L. Williams
     H.D. Lester

SECRET. SEPT 1918

1/1 HEREFORDSHIRE REGT.
102 Bde
34 DIV
B.E.F.

WAR DIARY
or
INTELLIGENCE SUMMARY.

Army Form C. 2118.

Place	Date	Hour	Summary of Events and Information	Remarks and references to Appendices
ST. OMER	1st	1330	SUNDAY. Orders to move. Bept moved Brigade at 10.00. Bn HQ personnel + 1 platoon per Coy entrained.	BELGIUM PARTS OF FRANCE Sheet 28 SW 1:20,000
		1415	Remainder of Bn marched off, proceeding to LUMBRES & entrained at 18.00, detrained at ABEELE at 23.45, dumped packs & marched to M 12 c 82 [SCHERPENBURG] & relieved 26 R.F. at 04.45.	
			Award of Immediate honors for July operations received [see APPDX]	
M 12 c 82 DIV RES.	2		Bn. proceeded to relieve 4 R.SUSSEX in front line N 24 c & c.85 N 23 & 47 & N 29 a & 73. Relief completed 04.30.	
FRONT LINE	3		Reorganizing front line, situation normal.	
"	4	04.30	Bn. formed up ready to move. 05.20 Artillery + M.G. barrage began.	
		05.34	Bn moved forward on objective, left being shell crater N 30.a. Right shell crater N 24 c.	
		07.00	Right Coy reached about N 30 a 27 & were held up by reverse (?) strands of barbed wire which had not been cut by our A/fire	
		08.00	Left Coy had failed to reach their objective & were back in FATINET Trench	

SECRET. Sept 1918

1st Herefordshire Regt
102 Bde
34 Div
B.E.F.

Army Form C. 2118.

WAR DIARY
or
INTELLIGENCE SUMMARY.
(Erase heading not required.)

Instructions regarding War Diaries and Intelligence Summaries are contained in F. S. Regs., Part II. and the Staff Manual respectively. Title pages will be prepared in manuscript.

Place	Date	Hour	Summary of Events and Information	Remarks and references to Appendices
FRONT LINE	4	0900	Right Coy had failed to break the M.G. nire back in original position except one platoon under Lieut J Wearmouth who held on to edge of crater when they maintained their position until dark then withdrawing to main line.	BELGIUM + Parts of FRANCE Sheet 28 SW 1:20,000
"	5	15.15	Right front Coy in touch with Bn on it's left advanced it's line to Boardman Trench + Patrols pushed out 200 in front. Patrols sent out to examine No Mans Land.	
"	6		Situation normal. Posts pushed out to N end of Oak Trench, Farmers Trench and N 29 b 3.7.	
"	7		Lt Col HM Lawrence DSO. to hospital. Major N F Chipp MC. assumed command.	
Res. N 15	8		Bn relieved by 1 Cheshire Regt moved to Res. position at Willeveck N 15 b 18. A very wet batch. No accomodation other than French + Boche old front line trenches.	
"	9		Raining trenches revetting head cover. Very wet day. 1st Reinfs rejoined	
"	10		Improvement of above continued. Bn on working parties under R.E. by day night. Lt Col E.B. Powell D.S.O. Rifle Bde assumed command.	
"	11		do for 1030 rain all day.	
"	12		do for 11th rain again.	
"	13			
M 16 & 10.7	14		Bn moved to M 16 & 10.7. French Bank, a much better area. Administrative work.	

SECRET   Sept 1918.   • **WAR DIARY** or **INTELLIGENCE SUMMARY**   • 1st Herefordshire Regt   Army Form C. 2118.

102 Bde   34 Div

Instructions regarding War Diaries and Intelligence Summaries are contained in F.S. Regs., Part II. and the Staff Manual respectively. Title Pages will be prepared in manuscript.

(Erase heading not required.)

Place	Date	Hour	Summary of Events and Information	Remarks and references to Appendices
Mt. 10.7	15		Bn relieved 2 L.N. Lancs Regt in front line, left sector, relief completed 2345.	Ref Map B + F Sheets 28 SW. 1:20,000
Div Res.	16		Lt Col E.B. Ross D.S.O. to hospital. Major W.J. Clapp M.C. assumed Command	
Front Line			(C. Coy) Left Front Coy pushed out posts about 150x went ahead at morning Stand to.	
"	17		(D. Coy) right front Coy pushed out posts to front of Oak Trench.	
"	18		Situation normal.	
"	19		Situation normal, posts pushed out + occupied craters in N.24. a.9.8.	
"	20		Situation unchanged, Bn relieved by 7 Cheshire Regt + moved to Support Line [Vierstraat].	
Support Line	21		Bn H.Qrs Siege Farm Shelled from 1400 to 1600 about 500 H.E. no casualties.	
"	22		Bn relieved by 1st R.W. Surrey Regt + moved to French Bank, 2320.	
Div Rest	23		Bn Admin + R.E. work.	
"	24		Do for 23rd.	
"	25		Platoon + section training musketry on 30x range.	
"	26		Do for 25th. Lt Col L.J. Caws arrived + resumed Command.	

"SECRET" SEPT 1918

Army Form C. 2118.

1st Hereford Regt 102 Bde 34th Div.

WAR DIARY
or
INTELLIGENCE SUMMARY
(Erase heading not required.)

Instructions regarding War Diaries and Intelligence Summaries are contained in F. S. Regs., Part II. and the Staff Manual respectively. Title Pages will be prepared in manuscript.

Place	Date	Hour	Summary of Events and Information	Remarks and references to Appendices
Div Res	27		Bn training. Drying up of strong feints.	Ref Map B + F Sheets 28 SW. 1:20,000
"	28		Under ½ hour notice to move.	
"		1900	Moved to Vierstraat	
Bde Res	29	0700	Moved forward in rear of 103 Bde, first to Green Line thence to about O.m.6.7 and occupied trenches. Lt Col Lyons to hospital. Major C.F. Chipp M.C. assumed command.	
"	30		Bn remained in present position.	

W.F. Chipp.
Major
Commg 1st Hereford Regt
30.9.18

War Diary Appendix
September 1918.

Drafts — 91 O.R.

Percentage sick to Hospital — 2½ %

Casualties

	Killed		Wounded		Missing	
	O.	O.R.	O.	O.R.	O.	O.R.
	2	14	2	83	1	17

Officers Joined

Lt Oakley P.J.	25.9.18	
Bell F.J.	25.9.18	
Chesney P.S.	25.9.18	
Milne	28.9.18	
Lt Col E.B. Powell	12.9.18	
Lt Col J.G. Lyons	25.9.18	Attached

Officers Evacuated

Lt Col A.H. Lawrence D.S.O. to Amb 7.9.18
    Struck off strength 21.9.18
    Authy. D.A.G.C.R No 60404/222/3
Capt L.W. Lewis to England 17.9.18
Lieut R. Bennett K in A 4.9.18
Lieut H D Lister " 4.9.18
Lieut A.C. Edwards Missing 4.9.18
Lt Col E.B. Powell (attached) to Amb 17.9.18
Lt Col J.G. Lyons (attached) " 30.9.18

SECRET.

Oct 1918.

1st Herefordshire Regt.
102 Bde.
34 Div.

WAR DIARY
or
INTELLIGENCE SUMMARY.
(Erase heading not required.)

Army Form C. 2118.

Instructions regarding War Diaries and Intelligence Summaries are contained in F. S. Regs., Part II. and the Staff Manual respectively. Title pages will be prepared in manuscript.

Place	Date Oct.	Hour	Summary of Events and Information	Remarks and references to Appendices
Wytchaete nr Houtem	1st	0900	Bn marched Brigaded to P.8.d.3.2 went into old sheds [enemy] for night.	Map Ref Sheet 28 S.E. 1/40,000
	2	0700	Bn moved to P.6.c central in reserve to 41 Div.	
		1930	Orders received to relieve 124 Bde in line from Q.4.C. central to Q.8.central. Bn in support, as there was no outpost Bn to relieve, Bn had to dig in, in approx Q.2.C. and d, very dark night, no guides available and no one who knew the ground. Bn dug in and when daylight came the position was found to be in rather dead ground.	
Support line	3		Situation normal. Usual harassing fire, positions selected for new outpost line.	
		1800	Bn proceeded to dig in, in selected positions in Q.2.C and d. Kept off 4 8 OR wounded.	
	4		Orders received to move, cancelled, work on defences continued usual Artillery fire. Situation normal.	
	5		Situation normal, usual enemy m.g. & artillery fire on area.	
	6		Orders received to relieve front line, then cancelled. Situation normal.	
	7	1930	Bn relieved by 2 Bn L. North Lancs about 1930 and proceeded by a cross country track to area about P.3.a.5.9, only a few Pill boxes available for shelter, nearly all ranks bivouaced in open.	

SECRET.

Oct/1918.

1st Herefordshire Regt.
102 Bde.
34 DIV.

Army Form C. 2118.

WAR DIARY
or
INTELLIGENCE SUMMARY.

(Erase heading not required.)

Instructions regarding War Diaries and Intelligence Summaries are contained in F. S. Regs., Part II. and the Staff Manual respectively. Title pages will be prepared in manuscript.

Place	Date Oct	Hour	Summary of Events and Information	Remarks and references to Appendices
DIV RESV P.3.a.5.9.	8		Resting and cleaning up.	Map Ref Sheet 28 S.E. 1/40,000
"	9		2 Coys working on roads under R.E. Coy Commdrs on reconnaissance.	
"	10		2 Coys working as for 9th.	
"	11		As for 10th.	
"	12		Orders received to relieve 2/4 R.W.S. in support line N Div Sector	
		1900	Bn moved off to effect relief in old support line.	
Support line	13		Situation normal.	
"		2100	Our Artillery carried out a gas bombardment of selected areas enemy replied.	
"	14	0535	ZERO hour. Bn in position ready to move.	
		0930	B & C Coys ordered to advance and consolidate YELLOW LINE.	
		1020	A & D Coys " = enemy gia front line.	
		1230	C Coy sent to reinforce 1/4 Cheshire Regt in front line.	
		1800	2 Platns of A Coy to support C Coy.	
		1900	Enemy shelled area continually. Still night with gas.	
			during night Coys consolidated their position.	
	15	0650	B Coy proceeded through the front line of 4th Cheshire Regt to eastern outskirts of MENIN, battle patrols pushed forward and cleared town after slight opposition. Coy followed & took up a line about R.14.d.8.8 to R.15.a.1.9 got into touch with 103 Bde on left	

SECRET.

1st Hertfordshire Regt
102 Bde
34 DIV.

Oct 1918

Army Form C. 2118.

WAR DIARY
or
INTELLIGENCE SUMMARY.
(Erase heading not required.)

Instructions regarding War Diaries and Intelligence Summaries are contained in F.S. Regs., Part II. and the Staff Manual respectively. Title pages will be prepared in manuscript.

Place	Date Oct	Hour	Summary of Events and Information	Remarks and references to Appendices
LINE	15	0900	C Coy ordered to take up a position about LOCK R.14.c.6.1	Map Ref Sheet 28.
"		1100	A Coy ordered to cover river from R.13.c.5.2 to R.19.a.3.8, D Coy to be in Res. about R.13.a.2.8.	
"		1800	Front line re-adjusted 4th Cheshire Regt withdrawn to support, Bn in touch with 103 Bde on left & 31 DIV on right.	
"	16	0100	Patrols sent out, one patrol sent to outskirts of HALLUIN, patrol after crossing L/Ls by means of the remains of MARATHON bridge, advanced 200x towards the Church, surprised an enemy M.G post and captured the gun, returning with it to river bank and getting it across by means of an enemy pontoon bridge, which the patrol found and swung across the river.	
"		0730	B Coy ordered to cross the river by means of the pontoon bridge and reinforce the 8 S.R. who had succeeded in reaching a platoon over to the HALLUIN side. As the 8 S.R. were unable to advance clear of the bridge head, being held up by M.G fire B Coy could not cross	
"		1200	A Coy ordered to cross the river about R.19.a.3.8 by means of a small raft constructed by from Duck boards [carrying 2 men] and worked by a party of the 4 Cheshire Regt, under cover of Artillery and rifle fire this Coy succeeded in getting across by 1600. As platoons crossed they advanced & cleared the	

SECRET.

1st Herefordshire Regt,
102 Bde
34 Div.

Army Form C. 2118.

Oct 1918

Instructions regarding War Diaries and Intelligence Summaries are contained in F. S. Regs., Part II. and the Staff Manual respectively. Title pages will be prepared in manuscript.

WAR DIARY
or
INTELLIGENCE SUMMARY.
(Erase heading not required.)

Place	Date	Hour	Summary of Events and Information	Remarks and references to Appendices
MENIN FRONT LINE.	16		enemy from buildings called RASCALS RETREAT. The Coy then dug in about R.19.a.6.1, 6.4.76 to hold the crossing. The crossing and subsequent advance was made under heavy enemy Artillery and M.G. fire. For 5 hours D Company worked at repairing the Lock & making a bridge about R.14.c.6.1 timber be having from the houses in MENIN during the whole time the position was shelled and sniped by the enemy. At about 1600 when the work was nearly completed the enemy opened a very heavy H.E. bombardment and destroyed the whole work.	Map Ref Sheet 28 1/40,000.
		1800	Bn was relieved by the 2/16 London Regt and proceeded to an area about K.35.	
BDE RES⟋	17		Adm St work & cleaning up. Lieut-Col Weldon arrived and assumed Command.	
	18		Coy and specialist training. Orders to be prepared to move.	
	19	0630	Bn marched Brigaded to R.H.a.2.5 to await orders	

SECRET

1st Herefordshire Regt
102 Bde
34 DIV.

Oct. 1918.

Army Form C. 2118.

WAR DIARY
or
INTELLIGENCE SUMMARY.

(Erase heading not required.)

Instructions regarding War Diaries and Intelligence
Summaries are contained in F.S. Regs., Part II.
and the Staff Manual respectively. Title pages
will be prepared in manuscript.

Place	Date Oct	Hour	Summary of Events and Information	Remarks and references to Appendices
ON MOVE	19	0930	Orders received, Bn moved thro LAUWE to M.15.c. Civilian population were greatly excited at the sight of British troops.	Map Ref Sheet 29 1/40,000.
		1400	Bn moved to HELBEKE M.29.	
		1700	Bn again moved to ST ANNE men accommodated in monastery.	
ST ANNE	20		Bn remained at 1/2 hours notice to move.	
	21		As for 20th	
	22		As for 21st	
ON MOVE	23	0800	Bn moved to about O.31.d ready to take over front line.	
		1800	Bn proceeded to relieve 23 RF in front line from about U.4.c central to O.28.d.1.7. relief completed by 2345.	
FRONT LINE	24	0215	In conjunction with the advance of the 123 Bde East of the Canal from about O.22 in a S.E direction B Coy were ordered to force the tunnel and Canal crossing about O.28.b.59 supported by C. Coy. As the 123 Bde did not advance the head of the crossing was not cleared & Bn did not press attack. B Coy dug in about O.28.c.3.10 and C Coy about O.28.c.3.3. remainder of day passed quietly.	
	25		In accordance with instructions Bn formed up in depth about O.28.b.4.8 West of Canal.	

SECRET

1/1st Herefordshire Regt
102 Bde
34 Div.

Oct 1918

WAR DIARY
or
INTELLIGENCE SUMMARY.
(Erase heading not required.)

Army Form C. 2118.

Instructions regarding War Diaries and Intelligence Summaries are contained in F. S. Regs., Part II. and the Staff Manual respectively. Title pages will be prepared in manuscript.

Place	Date	Hour	Summary of Events and Information	Remarks and references to Appendices
FIELD.	Oct 25		When barrage fell Coys closed up. As soon as 4th Cheshire Regt [who were on E bank of Canal and facing S.E] cleared the crossing about 0917 "A" Company went across by platoons to E bank of Canal but changed direction S.E. followed the reserve Company Cheshire Regt. The three remaining Coys followed Cheshire Regt in succession, the rear Coy being clear of the Canal crossing at 1015. Detail of Coys was:- "A" & "B" Companys in support of and in close touch with 4th Cheshire Regt. "C" Coy in rear of "B" detailed to follow and mop up the village of MOEN. "D" Coy to follow slowly in rear of "C" Coy and mop up area up to MOEN. There was no opposition at the crossing of the Canal, barbed wire in course of erection but not completed.	Map Ref Sheet 29 1/40,000
		1020	Enemy shelled crossing with 4.2's. By this time the while reaching the road crossing the railway at O.29.c.6.7 the reserve Coy 1/4th Cheshires there held up but M.G fire from left flank. "A" Coy brought up L.G to fire on the position with the desired effect, and the advance was resumed.	

SECRET.

1st Herefordshire Regt.
102 Bde.
34 DIV.

Army Form C. 2118.

Oct 1918.

WAR DIARY
or
INTELLIGENCE SUMMARY.
(Erase heading not required.)

Instructions regarding War Diaries and Intelligence Summaries are contained in F. S. Regs., Part II. and the Staff Manual respectively. Title pages will be prepared in manuscript.

Place	Date Oct	Hour	Summary of Events and Information	Remarks and references to Appendices
FIELD	25th		The advance was again held up by M.G. fire about O.29.d.2.6. This was again effectually dealt with by L.G's and advance continued. MOEN was under smoke barrage and enemy shell fire. One Coy 4 Cheshires were held up at house O.35.a.1.9. 2 Platoons B Coy went to assist, the house was captured and about 30 prisoners & 1 M.G.	Ref Map Sheet 29 1:40,000
"		1100	C Coy proceeded to clear village of MOEN, enemy having 2 M.G's on Eastern side village. These were dealt with and village reported clear 1258	
"		1400	Advance continued.	
"		1510	Bn was ordered to advance down E Bde boundary. Touch obtained with 41 Div on left	
"		1640	Bde having reached its objective, Bn proceeded to dig in as outpost about V.7.a and b and V.I.C. Enemy shelled area continually throughout the night.	
"	26		Bn remained in position.	
"		2230	Bn relieved and proceeded to + G.A arriving +	
MOVE	27	0900	Bn marched Brigaded to St ANNE men in horses and farms Lieut - Col. J.A. Muldon proceeded to command 1st R. Dublin Fus. Lieut - Col. E.H. Evans. M.C. R.W.F. arrived and assumed Command of Batn.	

SECRET.

Oct 1918.

Army Form C. 2118.

1st Herefordshire Regt.
102 Bde.
34 Div.

WAR DIARY
or
INTELLIGENCE SUMMARY.
(Erase heading not required.)

Instructions regarding War Diaries and Intelligence Summaries are contained in F.S. Regs., Part II. and the Staff Manual respectively. Title pages will be prepared in manuscript.

Place	Date Oct	Hour	Summary of Events and Information	Remarks and references to Appendices
MOVE	28		Bn marched Brigaded to B.23.d.6.7 were billeted in farms	Ref Map Sheet 29 1:40,000
"	29		Bn marched Brigaded to HARLEBEKE and occupied huts East of town.	
HARLEBEKE	30		Ordnry work. Coy training.	
"	31		As for 30th. B.G.C inspected 1st line transport.	

Army Burn
Lieut-Col
Comndg
1st Hereford Regt.

WAR DIARY APPENDIX October 1918

Drafts	38 O.R.		
Daily Sick % To Hospital	.66%	Total sick to Hospital for month of October	0 O 3 OR 162
Casualties	Killed 0 O 1 10	Wounded 0 OR 1 60	Missing Dies of Wounds 0 O 0 O 2 1
Officers Joined	2/Lt A.F. Mylne Lt-Col W.A. Meldon 2/Lt H. Devitt Lt A.R. Edwards A/Capt E.A. Evans M.C. 2/Lt J.W. Hunt		12.10.18 14.10.18 24.10.18 25.10.18 24.10.18 30.10.18
Officers Evacuated	Lt J.L. Bell Lt E.C. Gale Lt-Col C.A. Meldon Lt-Col J.G. Tyson Lt W.S. Bushell 2/Lt S.G. Ward Lt W.H. Hopkins 2/Lt L. Williams 2/Lt A. Birkmire 2/Lt A.L. Clarke 2/Lt C.D. Mitchell Lt J.G. Burdass	To Hosp. Wound (Acc) To Gas Div. To Hosp. To Hosp. Died of Wounds To England Killed in Action To England Wounded (Gas) To England Wounded (Acc)	26.10.18 26.10.18 27.10.18 30.9.18 8.10.18 10.10.18 10.10.18 15.10.18 26.10.18 11.10.18 12.10.18 14.10.18

SECRET

Army Form C. 2118.

1st Herefordshire Regt
34 Div.

WAR DIARY
or INTELLIGENCE SUMMARY.

(Erase heading not required.)

Nov 1918.

Instructions regarding War Diaries and Intelligence Summaries are contained in F.S. Regs., Part II. and the Staff Manual respectively. Title pages will be prepared in manuscript.

Place	Date Nov.	Hour	Summary of Events and Information	Remarks and references to Appendices
HARLEBEKE DIV Resv.	1		Coy training, L gun firing, musketry, specialist training as for 1st.	MAP. TOURNAI 1/100,000
"	2			
"	3	0800	Bn moved Brigaded to MOORSEELE, billeted in farms & houses.	
MOORSEELE Corps Resv.	4		Rest day. Bn concert in evening.	
"	5		Coy & Specialist training in further schools and games in afternoon. As for 5th. Memorial service, Anniversary of KRUWEILFEH.	
"	6			
"	7		Training as for 6th.	
"	8		Brigade succeeded to lines LYS near WEVELGHEM, practised construction of pontoon bridges, with canvas & trestles filled with straw, and fastened to boats. Bn crossed Rondelici bridge in 19 min. River at this point was 45' wide.	
"	9		Coy training. Presentation of British Colours (ribbons) to 34 Div the 11. Colls Embrick at WEVELGHEM	
"	10		Sunday. Bn Church Parade.	
"	11		Coy training. Hostilities ceased at 1100.	
"	12		Rest and games.	
"	13		Bde sports, following events won the Bn, 1st-Offs dismount, Tug o' war, 1st 320x, 2nd 440x, 1st Comp Jump, 2nd Regtl Jumps.	
ON MOWE	14	0800	Bn moved Brigaded to ROLLEGHEM, billeted in town.	
"	15	0800	Moved again to POTTES, billeted in scattered farms.	

SECRET.

1st HEREFORDSHIRE REGT

WAR DIARY
or
Nov 1918 INTELLIGENCE SUMMARY.

Army Form C. 2118.

34 DIV

Instructions regarding War Diaries and Intelligence Summaries are contained in F. S. Regs., Part II. and the Staff Manual respectively. Title pages will be prepared in manuscript.

(Erase heading not required.)

Place	Date Nov	Hour	Summary of Events and Information	Remarks and references to Appendices
ON MOVE	16		Bn moved Brigaded to RENAIX, Billeted in Convent.	MAP
RENAIX	17		Sunday Bde service in Convent yard.	TOURNAI 1/100,000.
ON MOVE	18		Bn moved Brigaded to FLOBECQ. Billeted in houses & school	
FLOBECQ	19		Resting & admit. work.	
	20		Coy training (Bns) in forenoon, games tc in afternoon.	
"	21		As for 20th.	
"	22		" 21st	
"	23		Bn [Hess&St] inspected by BGC 102 Bde.	
"	24		As for 22nd	
"	25		" " 24th	
"	26		" " 25th	
"	27		" " 26th	
"	28		" " 27th	
"	29		Bde inspected by GOC 34 DIV.	
"	30		As for 28th.	

Lieut. Col.
Commdg.
1st Herefordshire Regt

1st.Bn.The Herefordshire Regiment.

APPENDICES TO THE WAR DIARY FOR THE MONTH OF NOVEMBER, 1918.

APPENDIX 1. - CASUALTIES :

KILLED		WOUNDED		MISSING		SICK ADMITTED	
O.	O.R.	O.	O.R.	O.	O.R.	O.	O.R.
-	1	-	9	1	-	2	64

APPENDIX 2. - REINFORCEMENTS :

FROM ENGLAND		FROM HOSPITAL		VARIOUS		TOTAL	
O.	O.R.	O.	O.R.	O.	O.R.	O.	O.R.
6	-	1	125	2	1	9	126

APPENDIX 3. - OFFICER CASUALTIES :

```
2/Lieut.P.W.Chesney   - to hospital 1/11/18
Lieut.F.G.Burdass     - From Hospital 17/11/18
Lieut.C.T.L.Halford   - From England   "
2/Lieut.Leigh Bennett -    "     "     "
2/Lieut.G.D.Daniels   -    "     "     "
Lieut.C.R.Miles       -    "     "     "
Lieut.S.E.Knapp       -    "     "     "
2/Lieut.J.Ashmore     -    "     "   25/11/18
Lieut.H.A.Edwards     - To Hospital 29/11/18
Capt.E.V.Mullis       - From Base   17/11/18
Capt.T.R.Ginger       - From Base   20/11/18
```

ORIGINAL
"A" SECRET. DEC 1918. WAR DIARY 1st HEREFORDSHIRE REGT. Army Form C. 2118.
or
INTELLIGENCE SUMMARY. 34 DIV

Place	Date Dec	Hour	Summary of Events and Information	Remarks and references to Appendices
FLOBECQ	1		Brigade Church Parade.	Ret
"	2		Bn & Coy training	Mch.
"	3		as for 2 inst.	1,100,000
"	4		Bn Field.	TOURNAI
"	5		Bn route march	BRUSSELS
"	6		Bn & Coy training	NAMUR
"	7		as for 6th	
"	8		Brigade Church Parade.	
"	9		Bn drill	Approx.
"	10		Bn & Coy training	
"	11		Presentation of Belgian Foreign decorations by G.O.C. 34 Div to 10% Bde Group. [See Appx 1]	
			Bn marched to SILLY & new billeted in	
On Move	12		Buses & trains.	
SILLY	13		Rest day	
On MOVE	14		Bn marched to SOIGNES. Billeted in banway huts.	
SOIGNES	15		Sunday. Rest day. Bn Church Parade.	
On MOVE	16		Bn marched to LE HESTRE. billeted in houses	
			very wet march.	
	17		Bn marched to MONCEAU, billeted in empty houses	
On MOVE	18		Bn marched to CHATELET, billeted in empty factory.	
			Very wet march. Colors arrived from England. Wet march, brought through the lines! Capt O.B. Wallis, and Lieut. E. Jones.	

"SECRET"

WAR DIARY
or
1st HEREFORDSHIRE Regt — Army Form C. 2118.
INTELLIGENCE SUMMARY.
34th DIV

Dec 1918.

(Erase heading not required.)

Instructions regarding War Diaries and Intelligence
Summaries are contained in F.S. Regs., Part II.
and the Staff Manual respectively. Title pages
will be prepared in manuscript.

Place	Date	Hour	Summary of Events and Information	Remarks and references to Appendices
On Move	Dec 19		Bn marched Brigaded to FOSSE. Wet march. Billeted in empty houses	Ref MAP 1:100,000 NAMUR
FOSSE	" 20		Rearrangement + cleaning of Billets, this being the intended winter quarters	Or.
"	" 21		As for 20th	Or. Appx.
"	" 22		Sunday. V services. Suist. draft left to be demobilyed.	Or.
"	" 23		Admist. work.	Or.
"	" 24		As for 23rd.	Or.
"	" 25		X mas Day. Brigade Divine Service	Or.
"	" 26		Bank Holiday.	Or.
"	" 27		Bn route march.	Or.
"	" 28		Coy Training	Or.
"	" 29		Sunday. V.D. service	Or.
"	" 30		Bn + Coy training	Or.
"	" 31		Route March	Or.

Drinkwater
Lieut Col
Commdg. 1st Hereford Regt

1st.Bn.The HEREFORDSHIRE Regiment.

APPENDICES TO THE WAR DIARY for the MONTH of DECR.1918

APPENDIX 1. REINFORCEMENTS :

From Eng'd.		From Hospital		Various		TOTAL	
O.	O.R.	O.	O.R.	O.	O.R.	O.	O.R.
3			49	1		4	49

APPENDIX 2. CASUALTIES :

Killed		Wounded		Missing		Sick Admttd	
O.	O.R.	O.	O.R.	O.	O.R.	O.	O.R.
						2	56

APPENDIX 3. OFFICER CASUALTIES :

JOINED :- 2/Lieut.J.F.Brierley   From England 31/12/18
           2/Lieut.H.G.Perks   "   "   "
           2/Lieut.J.Bourne   "   "   "
           Capt.F.T.Nott   Reposted from 1st.K.S.L.I.
                                     Joined for Duty 21/12/18

QUITTED :- 2/Lieut.H.T.Avery   To Hospital 6/12/18
            2/Lieut.J.Jones   "   "   29/12/18

WAR DIARY
or
INTELLIGENCE SUMMARY

Army Form C. 2118.

1/Bn Herefordshire Regt.

Vol 8

(Erase heading not required.)

Place	Date	Hour	Summary of Events and Information	Remarks and references to Appendices
FOSSE BELGIUM.	1.1.19 to 10.1.19		Bath. company training. Platoon v company any football match. Bn cross country run.	OK5
	11.1.19		Divisional Commdr. Inspection.	OK5
	12.1.19		Voluntary Church Service. Bn. football match against A.S.C. Result Bn. 4 A.S.C.1.	OK5
	13.1.19		Bathing & internal administration. Capt Mullenstook over Bn. West Bourne leave.	OK5
	14.1.19 15.1.19		Bath & company training. First Round Bn. Commdrs Cup. Bath v. 2/4 Queens. Result Bath 2. Queens nil.	OK5
	16.1.19 18.1.19		Brigade Parade. Divisional Commdr. Inspection & Presentation of Medals to the Brigade followed by Inspection of Billets. Bath Concert party gave a performance during the evening.	OK
	19.1.19		Voluntary Church Service. Bn football match against 152 Bde R.F.A. Result R.F.A. 3 Bn 1. Concert party performed during the evening. 'D' Coy proceeded on detachment to MALONNE.	OK OK
	20.1.19 21.1.19		Bn training. Company football match. Officers v Sergts. Officers riding School.	OK
	22.1.19 23.1.19		Interior Economy. 'D' returned from detachment. Bath moves by train to GERMANY.	OK OK
BEUEL. GERMANY.	24.1.19 25.1.19		Bath relieved Canadian Bath. took over duties. Internal administration. Cleaning of billets & equipment.	OK OK
	26.1.19		Church parade in BONN CHURCH. Officers recconitred Bde outpost line.	OK
	27.1.19 to 29.1.19		Company training & education.	OK

Army Form C. 2118.

WAR DIARY
1/1st Herefordshire Regt.
or
INTELLIGENCE SUMMARY.
(Erase heading not required.)

Instructions regarding War Diaries and Intelligence Summaries are contained in F. S. Regs., Part II. and the Staff Manual respectively. Title pages will be prepared in manuscript.

Place	Date	Hour	Summary of Events and Information	Remarks and references to Appendices
BEUEL	30-1-19		Battn move to SIEGBURG.	OO5
SIEGBURG	31-1-19		Battn move to SEELSCHEID by motor lorry & took over left sub sector of COLOGNE BRIDGEHEAD. Lt.Col. EVANS MC returned from leave & resumed command of Battn.	OO5
SEELSCHEID				

Capt Evans ²⁄Lt CA
adj 1/1 Hereford Regt.

Appendices

Month ending Jan 31st

App I Casualties

Killed		Wounded		Missing		Sick Admitted		Total	
O	OR	O	OR	O	OR	O	OR	O	OR
-	-	-	-	-	-	1	22	1	22

App II Reinforcements

From Eng		From Hosp		Various		Total	
O	OR	O	OR	O	OR	O	OR
1	-	1	39	-	-	2	39

App III Officers Casualties

Lieut L Stokes from England.
2/Lieut G.D. Daniels to Hospital
2/Lieut G.D. Daniels from Hospital

34 Division
102 Infantry Brigade
1 Battalion Herefordshire Reg
Feb 1919 Missing

Army Form C. 2118.

WAR DIARY
or
INTELLIGENCE SUMMARY.

1/5th Hertfords. Regt.

(Erase heading not required.)

Instructions regarding War Diaries and Intelligence Summaries are contained in F.S. Regs., Part II. and the Staff Manual respectively. Title pages will be prepared in manuscript.

Place	Date	Hour	Summary of Events and Information	Remarks and references to Appendices
SIEGBURG.	1/3/19 to 2/3/19	—	Bath. Training. Route March. Inter platoon Football Competition.	&19.
	3.3.19	—	Gymnasium Classes morning & evening. Working parties & piquets at INGAR & ATHENRATH.	&19.
	4.3.19 to 10.3.19	—	Bath. Training. Divisional Cross country Run. Semi final. Inter platoon Competition.	&19.
	11.3.19	—	Officers v Sergeants football match result Sergeants 3 officers 2.	&19.
	12.3.19	—	Bath. Regtl. Church returned by 52nd Bedfords Regt. Bath Spank.	&19.
	13.3.19	—	Final Inter Platoon Football Competition. 1st Platoon to 5 Platoon won by 2 goals to 1. Bath reduced to a Cadre, which proceeded to the 34th Div. Reception Camp. Siegburg. All Volunteers & retainables of Officers & men proceeded to the 4th Suffolk Regt. at TROISDORF – B.E.F. 102 Officers addressed men prior to departure. Demobilizable men also proceed to Reception Camp with Cadre.	&19.
	14.8.19	—	50 O.R's left for U.K. for Demobilization.	&19.
	15.3.19	—	50 O.R's left for U.K. for Demobilization. Cadre & Remainder of O.R's for Demobilization were taken in Physical Drill & Games.	&19.
	16.3.19 17.3.19 18.3.19		Inspection. Physical Drill & Games.	&19.
	19.3.19		4 O.R. left for U.K. for Demobilization – Runner up & Phone.	&19.
	20.3.19 21.3.19		Inspection. Physical Drill & Games	&19.

Army Form C. 2118.

WAR DIARY
or
INTELLIGENCE SUMMARY. 1/1st HEREFORDSHIRE REGT

(Erase heading not required.)

Instructions regarding War Diaries and Intelligence Summaries are contained in F.S. Regs., Part II. and the Staff Manual respectively. Title pages will be prepared in manuscript.

Place	Date	Hour	Summary of Events and Information	Remarks and references to Appendices
SIEGBURG GERMANY.	22.3.19 23		Inspection. Physical Drill.	
	24			
	25			
	26		128. men left the monastery for U.K. for demobilisation, also Lieut Darrell.	
	27		Remainder of demobilisers men left the monastery for U.K. Bathing Parade. Pictures shows for men.	
	28			
	29		The Cadre left the Monastery Siegburg about 06.00 by lorries, & arrived at Cologne at 09-15	
	30		En route for Ath to join the 9th Div. (Very cold journey)	
ATH. BELGIUM.	31.3.19		Arrived ATH at 09-30. Billets and Cadre of Devon Regt.	

A. Halford Capt.
Comdg. 1/1st Herefordshire Regt.

SECRET.

WAR DIARY
or
INTELLIGENCE SUMMARY.

(Erase heading not required.)

Army Form C. 2118.

1st HEREFORDSHIRE REGT (CADRE)

APRIL 1919

Vol 11

Place	Date	Hour	Summary of Events and Information	Remarks and references to Appendices
				MAP REF:
ATH (BELGIUM)	1.4.19		First day after arrival from SEILBURG. Morning spent in arranging & cleaning billets	ATH (B.E.F.)
"	2.4.19	09.30	Billet Inspection. O games. Orders received to take over Unit Equipment of 2nd Bn. GT TOURNAI	GT 1:100,000
			DEVON REGT.	
"	3.4.19	09.30	Pullee Order Parade & Inspection. Fatigues (various)	
"	4.4.19	09.50	ditto	
"	5.4.19	09.00	All OR's of the CADRE inoculated. The COLLEGE BATHS ATH for bathing	
"	6.4.19	09.20	Billet Inspection - Pulvees Drill Parade.	
"	7.4.19	09.30	Drill Order Parade & Inspection - 6 men inspected for Guard Duty with the D.A.P.M. ATH	
"	8.4.19		Fatigues (various)	
"	9.4.19		"	
"	10.4.19		" Unit equipment of DEVON REGT finally taken over.	
"	11.4.19		"	
"	12.4.19		Bathing Parade at "College Baths" ATH.	
"	13.4.19	10.15	Divine Service. C. of E. service in Y.M.C.A. ATH. - Presbyterians & Non Conformist services held	
			in COURTS OF JUSTICE. GRAND PLACE. ATH	
"	14.4.19		Fatigues etc	

SECRET. WAR DIARY SHEET 2
or
INTELLIGENCE SUMMARY. 1/1st HEREFORDSHIRE REGT (CADRE)
APRIL 1919.
(Erase heading not required.)

Army Form C. 2118.

Place	Date	Hour	Summary of Events and Information	Remarks and references to Appendices
ATH (BELGIUM)	15.4.19		Y Fatigues etc.	MAP REF. TOURNAI 1:100,000
"	16.4.19		2ND BN. DEVON REGT (CADRE) entrained at 14.00 for DUNKIRK en route for U.K.	
"	17.4.19		Re-arrangement of billets etc. vacated by 2ND DEVON REGT	
"	18.4.19	10.30	(GOOD FRIDAY) Voluntary Church Parade in Y.M.C.A. (C of E only)	
"	19.4.19	09.00	Bathing Parade. Fatigues.	
"	20.4.19	10.30	Church Parade. Services for C of E, New Cons. & Presbyterians.	
"	21.4.19		Easter Monday. Holiday.	
"	22.4.19 to 26.4.19		Fatigues etc. (Nothing of interest)	
"	27.4.19	10.30	Church Parade. Services for C of E, New Cons & Presbyterians.	
"	28.4.19	10.30	Clothing Parade.	
"	29.4.19			
"	30.4.19		As for 26.4.19.	

Signed _____ Lt. Col
Comdg. 1/1st Herefordshire Regt.

www.ingramcontent.com/pod-product-compliance
Lightning Source LLC
Chambersburg PA
CBHW081247170426
43191CB00037B/2067